Pick Up the Poop Patrick

By
Thomas A. Schmidt
Color Illustrator
Omamori Kuro

Don't miss any of the latest releases of fun children's books
from Thomas A. Schmidt.
Join the Eye to Eye fan club Facebook group
to see behind the scenes on what it takes to create kid's books.

Patrick loved to play outside.
He enjoyed time with his best friends
Roxie and Sam and their dog
named Ranger.
They would ride bikes together
while exploring the neighborhood.
They played ball and went swimming
all summer long.

Patrick really wanted his
own dog. He would ask his
Mom and Dad
over and over again.
"I want a dog. I want a puppy.
PLEASSSSSE
can I have a pet?"
Every night Patrick
would dream of the perfect
pet playtime in the park.

Dad would listen and then ask,
"Can you be RESPONSIBLE
for the new pet?
Will you take care of it
and feed it and walk
it every day?"
Then he would add,
"Prove it by being responsible
and doing your chores
around the house!"

Patrick did not give up.
Every day he cleaned his room
and put away the dishes.
He helped Mom and Dad
even before they would ask.
Days passed and turned into weeks.
Then finally, Dad said
it was time to visit
the animal rescue to find the
perfect pup for Patrick!

What an exciting day
they had looking at all the puppies.
Patrick now had to find a name
for his little furry friend.
Should it be Rover, Rex or Ralph?
How about Barkly, Bear or Bruno?
Nothing sounded just right
so Patrick curled up next
to the pup for a quick nap.
When they both woke up
Patrick knew the perfect name.
It would be Winston!

Building a dog house
for Winston was the
first important project
for Patrick.
He and his buddy
Sam hammered and sawed
all afternoon long.
Slowly the puppy palace
came together.
Winston now had
his own little home.

Winston loved to run and play
with Patrick outside and through
all the rooms of the house.
Wintson also loved to chew
on things he was not supposed
to chew on! Dad's shoes,
Mom's magazines, and even
some of Patrick's favorite toys.
Puppies need to be trained
to have good family behavior.

A healthy pet is a happy pet.
Going to the veterinarian
for a check up is important
just like going to the dentist
is for growing children.

Patrick had lots of things he
needed to teach his new pet.
First, he needed to train his pup
not to chase other animals.
Winston loved to run and wanted
to chase everything that moved.
Squirrels, birds and cats.
Sometimes he would even
chase the neighbor's car!

One warm summer evening
Winston chased another critter
in the backyard.

Oh no!

It was a stinky skunk who did
not want to play along.
After being sprayed by the skunk
Winston smelled awful!.
Mom would not let him back in the
house until bath time
made the bad smell go away!

Food
WINSTON

Patrick's first RESPONSIBILITY
every morning was to make
certain Winston had plenty
of fresh food and water.
Just like little boys and girls,
all pets need lots of good food
to grow big and strong.

It's important for kids and pets
to get plenty of exercise every day.
Sometimes on a morning walk Winston
would have a little accident on
someone's lawn or sidewalk.
That's when Patrick would hear
his Mom shout,
"Pick up the Poop Patrick!"
That is why Patrick always brought
his proper pooper scooper bags to
clean up the doggy dodo.

Weekends were the best days
of the week for Patrick and Winston.
Saturdays often were swim time
to play at the lake!
They would take turns chasing
each other while jumping
off the end of the dock.
Winston never needed any lessons to
learn how to dog paddle.

After a fun day
of playing together,
bedtime would sneak up
on the active pair.
Before they would lay down
to sleep Mom would comb
out Patrick's messy hair
while Patrick would brush
Winston's furry coat keeping
it all shiny and clean.